Ta...

your Marriage

Take care of your Marriage

written by
Kass Perry Dotterweich

illustrated by
R.W. Alley

Abbey Press

Original title: Be-good-to-Marriage-Therapy
© Abbey Press, St. Meinrad, Indiana, USA
This edition distributed in Britain by
Powerfresh Ltd., 3 Gray Street, Northampton NN1 3QQ
Telephone 01 604 630 996 Facsimile 01 604 621 013
By consent of Libretto publishing (UK) Ltd., Leicester
Printed in England

Foreword

Since you were marrried, you and your partner have probably given careful attention to the practical aspects of your shared life: finances, children and their care, career goals, and home responsibilities. In the midst of all these concerns, however, it's easy to forget that love has a life of its own. Too often, couples neglect their relationship until tiny irritants grow into a serious crisis.

Be-good-to-your-marriage Therapy is a gentle attempt to help couples nurture love and head off troubles. The thirty rules in this book are gleaned from the sound advice of professionals and the tried-and-true experience of couples. The simplicity of the rules enshrines an ageless wisdom that can enable couples, through mutual respect, to live faithful to each other in the presence of God.

1.

Explore life together;
there's always something
new to discover.

2.

Ask for what you want; your partner can't read your mind.

3.

*Compliment your partner;
be sincere.*

4.

Compliment your partner in front of others; public praise lasts a long time.

5.

Touch your partner gently; touching says "I love you" in a special way.

6.

Be romantic; never stop courting each other.

7.

Respect your partner's right to privacy; individual space is important.

8.

Don't fear change; change in a marriage can mean growth.

9.

Spend time apart; separate interests generate interest between you.

10.

Play noncompetitive games together; you both win!

11.

Say "I love you"; it's a joy to hear those three little words.

12.

Always look your best; your partner deserves it.

13.

Fight fairly; no threats, accusations, or name-calling.

14.

Be willing to apologize;
love means being able to say,
"I'm sorry."

15.

Risk being hurt; love cannot deepen without risk.

16.

Graciously forgive; love is not proud.

17.

Entertain friends; they are part of your marriage.

18.

Laugh together; laughter can bridge great gaps.

19.

Cry together; shared tears bond hearts.

20.

Share your dreams; intimacy anticipates tomorrow.

21.

Surprise each other; the unexpected stirs the heart.

22.

Let yourself be weak; marriage is interdependence.

23.

Let yourself be strong; marriage is interdependence.

24.

Do loving things for your partner; your own heart will respond.

25.

*Respect your partner's family;
you're now part of it.*

26.

Look for love; it's there even when you don't "feel" it.

27.

Enjoy silence together; silence between lovers is sacred space.

28.

Remember the past; your past forms the present and the future.

29.

Pray; praise God for the life you share.

30.

Be patient with each other;
you're still getting married.

Kass Perry Dotterweich is managing editor of Triumph Books, an imprint of Liguori Publications. She and her husband, John D. Perry, are co-authors of the Elf-help Book *Friendship Therapy*. She has six children and lives in St. Louis, Missouri.

Illustrator for the Abbey Press Elf-help Books, **R.W. Alley** also illustrates and writes children's books. He lives in Barrington, Rhode Island, with his wife, daughter, and son.

The titles in the Elf Help series:

Be Good to Yourself
Without caring for your own needs, you will never be able to care for others.

Take care of your Marriage
Warm-hearted advice for couples who used to know all about love and romance, but may need a spark to rekindle the flame.

Enjoy your Womanhood
A celebration of the very special qualities that belong to one half of mankind.

Take it easy
Once in a while, it is all right to slow down, doing nothing much.

Celebrate your Birthday
Take pleasure in every candle on the cake, and be grateful for the life that you have been given.

Treasure your Friendships
A friendship should be nurtured and cared for in order to survive the strains and stresses of everyday life.

Saint Meinrad Archabbey, Abbey Press and Elf-Help

The first Elf-Help book, "Be Good to Yourself Therapy", was published in America by Abbey Press in 1987. This single title has now become a series, has been translated into several languages and has sold over 3 million copies!

Abbey Press is owned and operated by the Benedictine monks of St. Meinrad Archabbey. The series is the simple embodiment of the values of the Benedictine tradition.

The exuberant, sensitive and kind-hearted little elves were created by the illustrator R.W. Alley to help us appreciate what is truly important, and to value the miracle of life and the mystery of God's love.

With both wisdom and whimsy these cheeky little creatures with long noses teach us to respect others and ourselves and to embrace the fullness of life.